To my little Sun

Moumita Islam

BookLeaf Publishing

To my little Sun

Presentation by *BookLeaf Publishing*

Web: www.bookleafpub.com

E-mail: info@bookleafpub.com

ISBN: 9789357615501

First edition 2023

To my daughter, Mahreen, my little baby Sun.

To all the mothers out there enjoying the beauty of motherhood.

ACKNOWLEDGEMENT

I want to express my gratitude to my parents for their unconditional love for me and the hardships they endured while raising me. They are the foundation of everything I do and am. And I will always be grateful to my spouse, Mahodin, for his unwavering support.

INDEX

My Little Baby Sun

You are my little baby Sun-
Shining in my womb;
so bright and lovely you are!
in all your tiny little moves.

I love you, my little baby Sun-
Glowing inside my womb;
How humble and kind you are!
to adore your mother, hiding all of her dues.

You are my tiny baby Sun-
Dazzling in my womb;
So sweet and serene you are!
to lie deep in your mother's womb.

Oh, my little baby Sun-
I can wait no more!
I can see you coming!
Before the next coming dawn!
You will see my face and I will see yours!
That will be our day, and we will rock & roll.

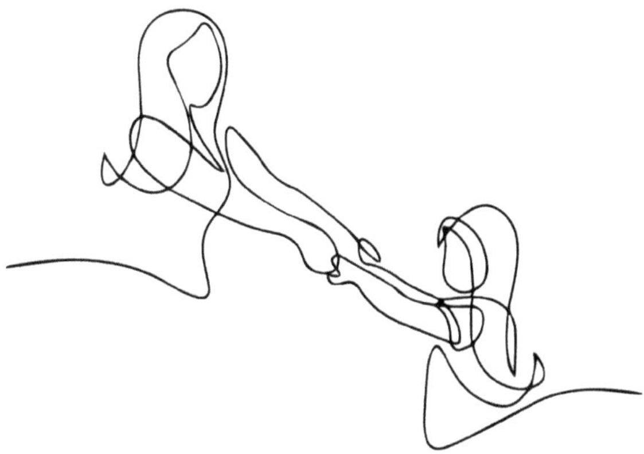

Rainy Morning

Rainy morning, rainy morning
Could you rain a little more?
Coffee brewing, coffee brewing
Don't you let us be alone!

Rainy morning, rainy morning!
Could you stay a little longer?
My little sun is in her sleep
Don't you leave her all alone!

Rainy morning, rainy morning!
Don't you be so sad at all!
My little sun will calm you down.
Once she puts her smile on!

Rainy morning, rainy morning!
Now my little sun is waking,
Take her to play a swing
The best of it will be yours.

My sun in the Ocean

You are wriggling inside, honey!
So I know I'm not here alone.
My bump is so cuddly to me these days.
I don't need anyone anymore!

You are calm at times, like the ocean across the sun.
And then you swirl like an approaching storm!
You twirl, you whirl, but you never know how to quit at all!
You struggle, you juggle, and you end up putting your big smile on!

You can hear me roar; I can see you soar.
Often, you become too tough, like a ball!
You jump too quick, drift so swift,
When you move on to strike the shore!

This is you, my brave sun-
digging all the sun rays up!
You do all this so the world can run
-like the brightest star ever!

My Little Sun Approaching

This pain is a pleasure for me, my love!
It does not hurt me at all.
My hun, you are so special to me.
I am waiting for that beautiful, lovely dawn!
That brightest day of my life!
It's approaching!

These nights will pass soon;
with all the pain and all the wounds.
The darkness of my womb will perish.
I am waiting for that pure and flourishing dawn!
That bright morning with my cuddliest sun!
It's approaching!

All the leaves are golden brown.
They are returning home,
so the new ones may come soon.
The wind is blowing all day long!
Fall is here, whispering in my ear now!
She is waiting for that magical dawn!
That dawn, with my beloved little sun!
It's approaching!

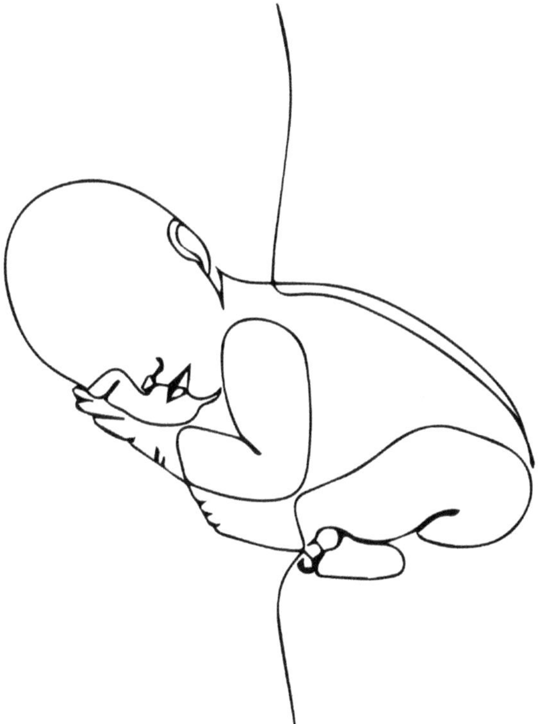

Baby Sun Counting her Days

Here is your baby seat;
Here is your bag!
We are all set for you;
let's march ahead!

I am your stroller, honey.
Ready to have fun?
All my wheels are there for you!
Let's set them on fire!

The baby's crib is all set,
calling you to her nest!
She is so jam-packed
for the winter coming ahead.

Baby baths in baby tubs,
so crucial now.
So you got two of them
to get washed around.

So many dresses, pink & purple,
ready to take you in their arms!
To cradle you in their lap, my honey!
they are waiting with open arms.

The old sun is now so jealous.
She won't let her sleep!
A curtain, dark and deep, comes home!
to let my baby sleep.

Now I smell a festive eve.
Our wait time is over indeed!
The pain will be so soothing, my honey!
For, that will make our baby sun smile.

No time to play

My little red sun has no time to play.
She brings back all that comes in grey.
The grass out there turns golden and gay.
To reach the whole world, she runs miles away.

She spins like a ball all day long!
She works so hard to please her mom.
When the evening steps on the floor,
she feels compelled to take a rest till dawn.

Is there any time to rest till dawn?
No, there's no time to rest till dawn.

The sun may set and wake you all,
but she can not stop a little at all.
When it is dark approaching to you,
someone puts on her morning shawl!

So my little sun has no time to play—
no time to sit, no time for delay!
She beams her light all day long.
Without a break the show must go on.

Chasing my Goal

Mama's little cuddly baby;
Papa's honey bun
I spread the shiny golden gleams
of a new beautiful sun!
Mama is my lighthouse;
Papa is my star.
I bring back all the clouds, so gloomy,
Dull, grey, and dark.

I shine so bright, red, and young
once I rise up,
To make the world look so vibrant,
beautiful, and warm.

Papa says to spread the light;
Mama says to flow.
They pray for their little girl-
to shine bright and grow!
Mama calls me a little sun
Papa a serene soul!
All their dreams come true the day
I start chasing my goal.

The Time has Come

The time has come!
Only you can feel it!
When your heart is waking you up!
You can see it coming!

And now you know,
This life couldn't be more beautiful!
As it's knocking that old sun out-
pouring life into the greens!

The leaves are nodding to the flowers,
The petals are peeping!
And all these remind me of you-
Our love! That old connection!

Could you feel the moves?
Could you feel the shifts?
keeping you all the way-
Beat, Beat, Beat!

No One out there

There is no one nearby-
only you and I!
Cuddling in the early morning sky,
with our lazy morning pie.

We make our breakfast;
we cook our lunch;
for no one out there,
to care for us.

We stroll and sit, yawn and read;
We get up and fall back asleep.
We cover in the dark and come out to light-
Since no one is there to hide & seek!

Because we love being alone,
And no one out there!
Thus, we make this bonding,
The sweetest one forever!

Little Sun talking to the Sky

I ask you, Daddy, where have you been?
Don't you see your little sun can spin?
She can see you now!

I can see you getting up and rushing through
Even earlier than the old lazy sun could do
Then you pray so long for me!
In the middle of the darkest dawn

Half asleep, half awake,
yet never late -
All that you do I know
you do it for ourselves.
That is how I see you, my daddy.
That is what makes you the best!
I am the proudest sun to rise
In her own sky, so brave.

I am not all alone
You are there with mom
I can not see you more often, though. yet can
feel us through each beat I play. .

You are the sky for your little sun to play.
so make sure there are no clouds on my way
Your little sun needs to shine and spray
All the happy beams of fay,
to make this world look more beautiful.

My cuddly bubbly mom

You are my lazy, busy mom.
You hold me so strong.
You are too tired to get on.
Yet, never give up and still carry on.

You are my sweet suttle mom.
I see you carrying me alone.
You've been waiting so long,
I'm right here with you, mom.

You are my cuddly, bubbly mom.
You think of me all day long.
There is so much stuff on.
But you hardly miss the one among all.

You are my honey bunny mom.
With a heart so kind and warm.
I see your tears rolling on,
for your love for me is so strong!

You love my daddy a lot.
But I know you love me the most.
As I am your little baby sun
growing inside your womb.
And no one else is from here
to love you so strong!

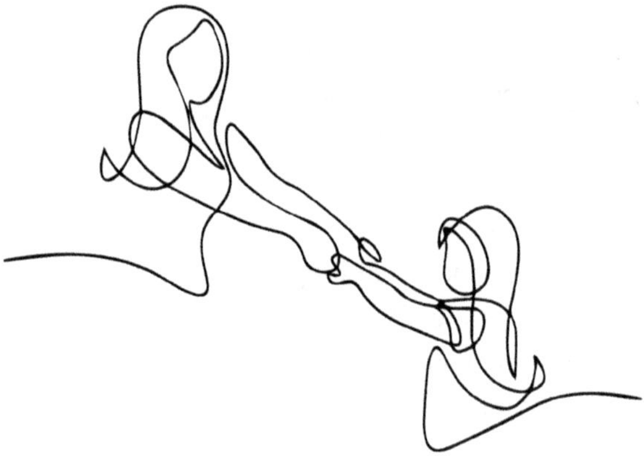

Our little sun joined the shore

No one else could count the pebbles on the shore.
It was you and me!
No one else could hear the silence and the roar!
It was you and me
The drops of sweat we sifted and crafted into the soul.
We rafted together and are still rafting on our vows.

But we are stronger than before!
Our little sun has joined the shore.

She's holding our hands in the middle of chaos.
And all our worries have gone to the gallows.We three
are chained like a girdle, so bold.
None can break us till the sun goes past its glow.

we met us late

We could become us-
before the sun had met the earth.
We could become us-
before the sky had put on her winking stars.
Before the moon had ever learned to rule her
beholder's heart,
Could we not become us?

Now It's too late!
The time has stepped in between
to lead us all to death.

I wish we could be there before that eternal fate.
Now it's too late.
For now, time will tie us to life so short.
We won't have time to love or r adore.

I wish we could become us.
a little before, honey.
to make this bond an eternal ethos.
But now it's too late.

The light inside

Before you go and grab all the lights of the show,
I warn you, my love.
You might end up soon with nothing to glow.
There is no such thing there to lift up your soul!

Before you leave for the lights across the sea,
I tell you, my love.
This might be a splash of mirage in your eyes.
There is no such thing there to strengthen your hopes.

You better stay here, on this side of the shore.
In the middle of darkness, where no one else can roar!
Lonely yet lively,
Like these mysterious ripples in the flow!
She has no light of her own-
Yet dazzling in the splendor of reflection!

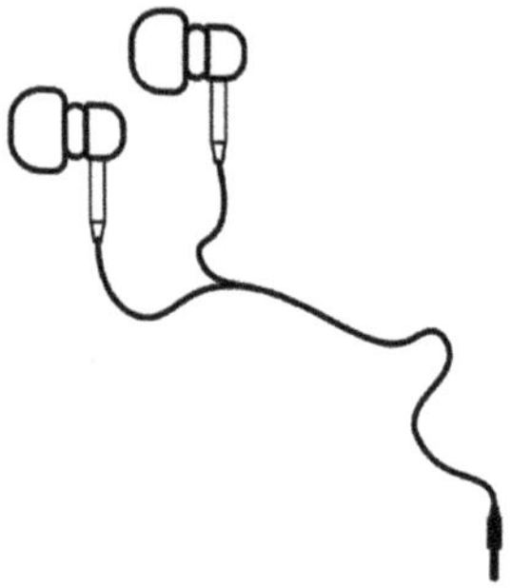

Little sun on her way Home

Head down, legs up;
I am now mommy's big girl!
I have two enormous eyes to see,
All of this upside-down world!

Though it seems like a big blurry bowl

A gloomy sun a foggy moon and nothing more!—
But I can see them doing all my stuff alone.
They are in a rush as I have little time in her womb.
I am coming to be your best little kid, for sure.
I will be the strongest to save my world and more.

Why, Dear Mommy, have you never asked me why-
I am rushing to be outside and make you cry?
Then I could tell you my story-
that I have to strive for us;
and make things right for you.
that I have to thrive on justice
to make the world turn around

Dear Mommy, your womb is so warm for sure, But I can't wait here anymore.
Let the new sun come up on the shore
So she can shine upon her beauty and roar!

Time, I beg you now

Time is ticking away
I'm here alone, standing.

I beg you, dear time; I beg you now.
Wait, a little while longer, because
I have the desire to cover you off.
For I will look into the future now,
to see my little sun's face.

Time, could you see my words?
all covered in silence!-
Hanging across the river, panting!
A baffling murmur!
Could you hear it?

The sky's shouting its silence across the sky.
Unheard, cluttered words-
crawling towards a beautiful tie
like a starlit sky
with no stars on it;
still gliding!

Let me glide on you like that, dear time.
For I can't wait to unveil you now,
And hear my baby sun cry!

I'm sorry

It's 12:06 am on October 10.
I'm still waiting for sleep.
Is it chilling outside, honey? Perhaps not!
It's our fever killing us inside,
and I am sorry.

Is it too tough for you, baby?
Maybe it is, and I am sorry

But I know you are the strongest.
You will get through all this.

We will get through this together.
None can stop us from seeing each other.
We are going to meet soon, my honey.
That day is not very far away.

Yet, it hurts inside, honey, and I am sorry.

We won't Fall apart

Dear Mommy, don't fall sick.
I will be there in a few weeks.
You should not become tired or weak.
My sweetest momma is forever so sweet

I know I'm too heavy for you!
Too heavy to walk; too heavy to move!
I'm trundling slowly yet stronger than before,
A big kid I am now with a small room for sure!

No matter how tough it is!
We will fight it all.
Baba is always there for us.
He will never let us fall.

Dear Momma, Don't cry a bit.
Allah's there for us to see.
He is so kind and merciful in His deeds.
We will rise gracefully, indeed!

Printed in the USA
CPSIA information can be obtained
at www.ICGtesting.com
LVHW081243021223
765302LV00011B/180

9 789357 615501